Castruccio Castrucani by Letitia Elizabeth Landon

OR, THE TRIUMPH OF LUCCA

Letitia Elizabeth Landon was born on the 14th August 1802 in Chelsea, London.

A precocious child she had her first poem published is 1820 using the single 'L' as her marker. The following year her first volume appeared and sold well. She published a further two poems that same year with just the initials 'L.E.L." It provided the basis for much intrigue.

She became the chief reviewer of the Gazette and published her second collection, 'The Improvisatrice', in 1824.

By 1826, rumours began to circulate that she had had affairs. For several years they continued to circulate until she broke off an engagement when her betrothed, upon further investigation, found them to be unfounded. Her words reflect the lack of trust she felt "The mere suspicion is dreadful as death"

On June 7th 1838 she married George Maclean, initially in secret, and a month later they sailed to the Cape Coast.

However, the marriage proved to be short lived as on October 15th, that same year, Letitia was found dead, a bottle of prussic acid in her hand.

Index of Contents

INTRODUCTION
DRAMATIS PERSONÆ
SCENE: In Lucca, Italy
CASTRUCCIO CASTRUCANI
ACT I
SCENE I—A Market-place
SCENE II—The Senate-house
ACT II
SCENE I—Apartment in the Arrezi Palace
SCENE II—Interior of a Church
ACT III
SCENE I—A Banqueting Hall opening into a garden, and hung with pictures
SCENE II—A small Chamber looking to the Street
SCENE III—A Hall in one of the Palaces
ACT IV
SCENE I—The same Hall as before, but now illuminated, hung with Pictures, &c.
SCENE II—Part of a Garden
ACT V
SCENE I—A Prison
SCENE II
SCENE III—The Market-place

INTRODUCTION

The scene is laid in Lucca, during the contests between the Guelphs and the Ghibellines; but my object has not been to bring forward old party distinctions, in which no one now takes any interest, but to represent the first rising against the feudal system, which has since led to such important results. Castruccio is the (attempted) ideal of the hero and the patriot. He has himself been exiled and oppressed; out of this early experience grows his sympathy with the wrongs of the city to whose cause he devotes himself, while the glory of Lucca is the poetry and passion of his life. Count Leoni is merely one of a faction, referring all things to small and individual interests. He is the representative of the few, while Castruccio is that of the many.

DRAMATIS PERSONÆ

MEN
Castruccio Castrucani—Leader of the popular party in Lucca.
Count Gonsalvi—Envoy from Florence.
Count Arrezi—one of the secretly opposed Nobles.
Count Leoni—his Nephew, just returned from travel.
Cesario—Secretary to CASTRUCCIO
Nobles, Citizens, Soldiers, &c.

WOMEN
Bianca—Daughter of Count Arrezi, betrothed to CASTRUCCIO
Claricha—an orphan dependant in the house of ARREZI
Ladies, Attendants, &c.

SCENE: In Lucca, Italy.

CASTRUCCIO CASTRUCANI

ACT I

SCENE I —A Market-place.

CITIZENS grouped together, talking earnestly.

1st CITIZEN
How was he taken? for he would have fought

A dozen single handed.

2nd CITIZEN
Last night, returning from the Count Arrezi,
To whose fair daughter he has been betrothed,
He was surrounded by those foreign bandits
That wear Count Ludolph's colours.

1st CITIZEN
Work fitting to their mercenary hands.

2nd CITIZEN
I saw the whole, for I was late at work.
Castruccio pass'd me as I hurried home;
Dark as it was, I knew his stately form!
He cross'd the street, and out of ambush sprung
The secret enemy. I saw him fling
His cloak upon the ground—out flash'd his blade—
But the dark night was lit with glittering steel,
And twenty swords were drawn to meet but one.
I heard the clash, then a fierce struggle—oaths—
And he was hurried past: the moon shone out,
And there lay on the ground a broken sword,
But red with blood.

[Enter CESARIO

1st CITIZEN
Here comes his young and trusted officer,
The Count Cesario; he will tell us more.

2nd CITIZEN
What of Castruccio's fate—what of our chief?

CESARIO
The treachery of the nobles has prevail'd.
Castruccio lies within the city prison,
Thither convey'd by Ludolph's foreign band;
A thousand dangers circle him around,
The secret dagger, and the open scaffold.

2nd CITIZEN
Well, now we have no friend!

CESARIO
He was your friend; the meanest citizen
Found, in the shadow of Castruccio's name,
His best security.

2nd CITIZEN
He never wrung from us our hard-earn'd gains.

1st CITIZEN
Our lives were precious to him; must he die?

2nd CITIZEN
The nobles are too strong.

CESARIO
'Tis for your sake they are his enemies.
He might have shared their power, and kept ye slaves.

2nd CITIZEN
We have been much oppress'd; until he came,
No one could sit in quiet at his door.
Money and blood were the perpetual cry
Of our small tyrants.

CESARIO
So will it be again,
If your protector perish.

ALL
He shall not die!

CESARIO
The nobles will not listen to your prayers.

1st CITIZEN
We will try threats.

CESARIO
Threats are as vain as prayers—ye must try deeds.

2nd CITIZEN
What can we do? We are unarm'd and weak!

CESARIO
But strong in your good cause. Oh, ye are strong,
If ye would know your strength!

2nd CITIZEN
When he was free, we could defy the world.

CESARIO
Then give him what ye owe him—liberty.

2nd CITIZEN
All Lucca will rise up!

1st CITIZEN
Before this, I have fought upon his side;
Up! let our watch-word be Castruccio's name.

CESARIO
Let the high Heaven hear it; will ye stand
Meek, pitiful spectators of his death?

2nd CITIZEN
The nobles will not shed Castruccio's blood.

1st CITIZEN
When have they been so merciful to spare?

2nd CITIZEN
They will not spare from mercy, but from fear.

CESARIO
Who should they fear?

2nd CITIZEN
The oppress'd and desperate.

CESARIO
Not if oppression find relief in words.

1st CITIZEN
There's not a street in Lucca but should run
Red with our blood before Castruccio die!

CESARIO
'Tis well, if ye dare act upon these words.

ALL
We dare.

CESARIO
Let each one to his neighbours instantly;
Gather what force ye can; by two and threes
Return, and then we'll try the prison's strength.

2nd CITIZEN
Three of the nobles come this way.

CESARIO
We must disperse until the hour arrive,
What time the nobles seek the Senate-house.

2nd CITIZEN
Where they will meet to doom Castruccio's death.

CESARIO
Short space is ours, be silent, and away.
In one half hour seek ye the market-place;
Castruccio Castrucani is the word.—

[Exeunt.

[Enter **NOBLES**.

1st NOBLE [Putting two of the **CITIZENS** aside]
Out of the way, ye loiterers.

2nd NOBLE
What do ye here, wasting what ye call time,
And then complain of want?

1st CITIZEN [Aside]
Our time will come.—

[Exit.

1st NOBLE
What said the knave?

2nd NOBLE
Good saints, I know as little as I care.
I do not share Castruccio's sympathy
For those who are the dust beneath my feet.

1st NOBLE
'Tis pity of him; for more gallant knight
Ne'er led the foremost, still himself the first.
I grudge the yielding to the Florentines
That now must follow.

2nd NOBLE
Better submission to the distant power
Than that within our gates; the citizens,
Stirr'd by Castruccio, talk of their rights:
Time was, a creditor, grown troublesome,
Might hang, a useful warning, at our door;

But Castrucani has so changed the state,
That not a knave who walks the market-place
But holds his life as precious as our own.
Why Lucca is as quiet as a bower.

1st NOBLE
We have had stirring times outside our walls,
Victory on victory o'er the Florentines.

2nd NOBLE
And this has dazzled ye: ye have not mark'd
How stronger, hour by hour, has grown his sway.
Among ourselves, if it were left to him,
We should not have a single privilege
Beyond the meanest citizen.

[Enter the **COUNT LEONI**, as if from a journey, speaking to his **PAGE** as he enters.

See all your charges safe: then follow me,
Bringing the casket where my cousin's name
Is work'd in pearls.

1st NOBLE
Welcome again to Lucca, Count Leoni

[**ALL** gather round him.

LEONI
Kind greeting to you all: I am right glad
To see my friends and native walls again.

2nd NOBLE
You're come upon us in a stirring time.

1st NOBLE
Tell him at once Castruccio is our prisoner.

2nd NOBLE
You're over hasty; for the count may be
One of Castruccio's partisans.

1st NOBLE
Arrezi always liked the strongest side,
And hence betrothed his daughter to Castruccio.

LEONI
What, to my cousin—to the fair Bianca?

1st NOBLE

You do not look as if you liked the news.

2nd NOBLE

Will you go with us to the Senate-house?
Your uncle will be there.

LEONI

As yet I am too new to join your councils.

2nd NOBLE

We may not loiter, even now awaits
The envoy sent from Florence.

LEONI

Make ye what terms ye can—secure yourselves:
The Florentines will gladly aid your cause.
They hate Castruccio—hate, because they fear.

2nd NOBLE

We are too late: farewell, we meet anon.[Exeunt.

LEONI [Solus]

Well, fortune, thou hast stood my friend at last!
I came to struggle with mine enemy,
And, lo! he is subdued. Castruccio lies
A prisoner at the mercy of his foes.
For him there is one only ransom—death!
Soon will these hasty nobles want a head:
The power and wealth of our most ancient house
Point to Arrezi as the nobles' chief,
And he will be a cypher in my hands.
Now will my secret trafficking with Florence
Stand in good stead: my path is clear before me.
The odium of the Castrucani's death,
And the inglorious peace they now must make,
Rests with the nobles. Fortune, now thy tide
Is on the turn—I dare to ride thy waves.
Strange that Castruccio, who through life has been
My too successful rival, now should make
My first step in the ladder of ambition.
Now must I seek my cousin, fair Bianca,
So nearly lost; how will she greet me now?
Castruccio's sway has been right absolute,
Or never had Arrezi let his child
Link with our house's ancient enemy.Exit.

The Senate-house

COUNT GONSALVI, COUNT ARREZI, NOBLES, ATTENDANTS, &c.

GONSALVI [Taking a seat]
Henceforward Florence claims your fealty;
She will secure you in all ancient rights,
Immunity, and privilege: her sword
Will stand between ye and your enemies.
For this a yearly tribute must be paid
Of twenty thousand florins.

2nd NOBLE
Our treasury's low, my lord.

GONSALVI
And so is ours,
Exhausted by the late vexatious war.

2nd NOBLE
Urged by the Count Castruccio, not ourselves.

GONSALVI
It must be paid.

2nd NOBLE
Well, well,
The goldsmiths round our market-place are rich.
The citizens, too, better being poor,
As more obedient, right that they should pay
The penalty of their rebellious spirit.

GONSALVI [Rising]
I leave you till to-morrow, when I bring
The treaty ready for your signatures,
And will receive your homage and your oaths.—

[Exit.

1st NOBLE
Homage and tribute—these are bitter words!

2nd NOBLE
Less bitter than the Castrucani's sway.

1st NOBLE
To-day must fix his fate. What is his doom?

SEVERAL NOBLES
Death!

ARREZI
Rather say exile.

2nd NOBLE
Yes, and one week sees him again our chief!

ARREZI
He may be kept strict prisoner.

2nd NOBLE
And keep perpetual terror o'er our heads.

SEVERAL NOBLES
His scaffold is our safety.

ARREZI
We dare not raise that scaffold.

SEVERAL NOBLES
Dare not!

ARREZI
The citizens would rise in his defence.

1st NOBLE
Not with our swords to teach them what they are.

2nd NOBLE
Why risk a tumult that we well may spare,
While Lucca has a dagger?

1st NOBLE
He shall not perish by the assassin's hand.

2nd NOBLE
So that he perish, little matters how.

ARREZI
The tumult would be fearful.

1st NOBLE
Even now

The people gather fiercely in the streets.

2nd NOBLE
Let them not see him, they will soon forget.

ARREZI
Hark to the shouts!

1st NOBLE
I have a useful knave, who, give him gold,
Stabs and forgets; I'll send him to the prison.

2nd NOBLE
The noise approaches, look ye to your swords.

1st NOBLE
Delay is fatal—let Castruccio die!

[While he is speaking the doors are burst open, and **CASTRUCCIO** enters, armed and attended.

CASTRUCCIO
Not yet, nor by your hand! Thanks, gentlemen,
For an indifferent lodging. I have learnt
That prisons, tenanted with thoughts of death,
Is not a punishment to order lightly;
Therefore, ye shall not fill my vacant place.

2nd NOBLE
The game is yours—I, for one, ask not mercy!

CASTRUCCIO
And, therefore, worthier to have unask'd.
Ye do mistake me, signors: all my thoughts
To ye are grateful ones. But for your rash
And ill-advised attempt, I had not known
How true the love on which my power is built—
How strong the cause the people trust with me!

[Re-enter **COUNT GONSALVI**.

GONSALVI
I must demand some escort: for the streets
Are fill'd with people, and unwillingly
Would I shed blood. What! Castrucani here?

CASTRUCCIO
Ready to give the Count Gonsalvi audience,

And ask, what are the terms he brings from Florence?

GONSALVI
With these, the representatives of Lucca,
I have arranged our treaty.

CASTRUCCIO
On what terms?

GONSALVI
That ye submit yourselves, and pledge your faith
True vassals unto Florence: and each year
Remit your tribute—twenty thousand florins!

CASTRUCCIO
Tribute and homage! can they sink so low,
Men who have met ye bravely in the field?
Now hear me, Count Gonsalvi: Lucca rather
Would see her walls dismantled, than consent
To yield such base submission!

GONSALVI
These are her chiefs—in their consent she yields.

CASTRUCCIO
You see that they are silent. By my voice
Does Lucca speak: she would be glad of peace,
An equal, sure, and honourable peace—
To terms like these she has but one reply—defiance.

GONSALVI
Florence will teach you better in the field!

CASTRUCCIO
This to your conqueror: not three weeks have pass'd
Since, in the field, we met. I think you found
More service from your spurs than from your swords.

GONSALVI
'Twas an unlucky chance of war.

CASTRUCCIO
Not so, my lord; there was a higher cause—
The right against the wrong. Your army came,
A mercenary and a selfish band,
Some urged by false ambition, some for spoil.
No noble motive noble impulse gave:
Ye were aggressors, and ye fought like such.

I tell you, count, with not a third your numbers
I chased your flying hosts within your gates.

GONSALVI
I came not for a boast but for an answer—
War or submission.

CASTRUCCIO
War or submission! sad such choice and stern:
Vast is the suffering—great the wrong of war!
But—and all Lucca speaketh in these words—
Rather we take the suffering; and the wrong
Rests on the oppressor's head, than we submit.
Not while one hand can strike on Lucca's side,
Not while one stone is left of Lucca's walls,
Not while one heart beats in our country's cause,
Will Lucca stoop beneath a foreign yoke.
Ye only fight for conquest or for spoil:
We for our homes, our rights, our ancient walls!
The sword is drawn—God be the judge between us!

GONSALVI
Have ye no other answer?

CASTRUCCIO
None! Cesario is your escort to the gates.

GONSALVI
I take your answer—war, then, to the death.—

[Exit.

2nd NOBLE
Are ye not rash in this? how weak our state,
Compared with Florence.

CASTRUCCIO
Twice have we met them in the open field,
Each time they fled before us. Oh! my friends,
If I may call ye such, we are not weak
Who have our own good swords, and urge a war
Just in the sight of heaven. Our weakness lies
In our dissension, in the small base aims
That disunite us from the common cause.
Lucca were strong, had Lucca but one heart!
Why should ye be mine enemies? I seek
Yours in the general good. I stand between
Ye and a people whom ye would oppress.

Know ye not, love has stronger rule than fear?
A country, fill'd with tyrants and with slaves,
What waits upon her history?—crime and shame!
But the free state, where every rank is knit
By general blessings, freedom shared by all,
There is prosperity—there those great names
Whose glory lingers though themselves be gone.
It is not I ye serve, it is your country!—

[Applause.

2nd NOBLE [Aside]
I see that we must yield, or seem to yield;
He's master now.

CASTRUCCIO
And for this base submission
To your hereditary enemies,
There is no yoke so galling as the yoke
Foreign invaders place upon your neck!
The heavy and the arbitrary sway
That ye would fix upon your countrymen,
Would soon be on yourselves. Lucca is free;
To keep her so is trusted to your swords!
I march to meet the Florentines to-morrow;
Will ye not follow me for Lucca's sake?

NOBLES
We will.

CASTRUCCIO

Now must I forth to thank the citizens.
[Sees **ARREZI**]
The Count Arrezi here!

ARREZI
I came here as your friend.

CASTRUCCIO
Then bear but hence my greetings to your daughter.

ARREZI
My lord, she is much honour'd!

[Shouts without.

CASTRUCCIO

The people are impatient, let us forth:
I am impatient, too, to thank their love.
We will go forth together, and with them
Make common cause.

[Exeunt.

SCENE I —Apartment in the Arrezi Palace.

CLARICHA [Seated at an embroidering-frame]
The past it is my world: ah! but for that,
How could I bear the present? In the past
Is garner'd all most precious to my soul.
It is not true that love decays or dies
With time or absence: years have pass'd away,
Yet still my dreams are faithful to one thought.
One voice makes secret music in my ear,
Distinct as when it breathed its earliest vow.
Long since hath hope grown faint, but weary never!
Fate may have said that we shall meet no more!
But rather would I live upon the love
Whose only food is memory, than forget,
And ask oblivion for its cold content.

[Enter **LEONI**.

LEONI
Nay, I must not disturb you: pray resume
Your graceful task.

CLARICHA
Pardon me, sir.—

[Going—he detains her.

LEONI
'Tis long since I have seen so fair a face,
And cannot part with it so readily.

CLARICHA
I will announce your coming to my lady.

LEONI
She knows it, sweet, and will be here anon.

The time will not seem long with those dark eyes
To count the minutes by.

CLARICHA
You must excuse my stay.

[Snatches her hand from him—exit.

LEONI [Solus]
Women exaggerate all things—most of all
Our flatteries and their power. Foolish girl!
She might have pass'd my waiting pleasantly.
But soft! here comes my uncle.

[Enter **ARREZI**.

ARREZI
Welcome, fair nephew, once again to Lucca.

LEONI
Thanks, my kind kinsman; but, before I say
A word of greeting, tell me of your news.

ARREZI
This 'twixt ourselves—I bring the very worst.
Castruccio is again the lord of Lucca.

LEONI
It cannot be.

ARREZI
The people rose and freed him from his prison,
Bore him in triumph to the senate-house,
And, once among us, all gave way before him.

LEONI
What! did ye yield, so many as ye were?

ARREZI
What could we do? strong as the angry sea,
The people gather'd fiercely at the gates,
And many of the younger nobles lean'd
Towards his side, chafed at the thoughts of peace
Bought by submission to the Florentines.

LEONI [Aside]
Cowards and traitors to themselves.
[Aloud]

And now
What is the course ye mean to follow?

ARREZI
Our power is broken, and we must submit.

LEONI
Is it the head of our most noble house
Who names submission to the Castrucani?

ARREZI
What can we do? he's brave and eloquent.
His sword subdues the Florentines, his tongue
Enchants the people!

LEONI
What can ye do?—resist.

ARREZI
What has resulted from our late resistance
But a more firm assurance to his sway?

LEONI
Fools, that could let a prison stand between
Their enemy and death!

ARREZI
We must conciliate now.

LEONI
He is to wed
The fair Bianca.

ARREZI
We shall share his power.

LEONI
I like no sharing but the lion's share.
This was not once the temper of our house:
The Castrucani owed their banishment
To us and ours.

ARREZI
Ah! those were glorious days.
None question'd, then, our rightful sovereignty.

LEONI
Which half the citizens now laugh to scorn.

As yet I have not been an hour in Lucca,
Yet I can see all things are changed.

ARREZI
Too true!

LEONI
Your servants are your masters; where are gone
Your old respect and high authority?

ARREZI
I do not know the times in which I live.
So much of change lies heavy on each hour!
Castruccio comes to-night—now greet him fair.

LEONI
What! when he comes a suitor to my cousin?

ARREZI
Such an alliance will secure us all.

LEONI
I tell you, count, that it shall never be;
Think upon what you owe your ancient line:
Its feuds are bonds its honour must hold dear.
We hate the Castrucani!

ARREZI
I have small cause, if you knew all, to love them.

LEONI
And yet you yield and tamper with Castruccio.

ARREZI
And once again, I say, what can we do?

LEONI [Aside]
He wavers—ancient hatred is too strong
For the new bond of interest and of fear,
But yet I dare not trust him with the scheme
That rises dark and vague upon my mind.
I must think more.
[Aloud]
—Again, I say, resist!
But wisely, calmly; never should the sword
Flash till it strikes.

ARREZI

I'll tell you truly, kinsman,
I like not this alliance: it is forced
On us by evil days and evil fortunes.
Now, more than ever, do we need such aid,
For I misdoubt but that Castruccio knows
'Twas not to serve him that I sought the council
When he was prisoner.

LEONI
Bid him, as you said,
To a gay banquet here, and bid with him
All his chief followers; let us seem friends:
And, if we watch our hour, that hour will come.

ARREZI
I'll to the Castrucani palace straight,
And urge our welcome.

[Exit.

LEONI [Solus]
And he will come; danger escaped but makes
The brave more daring; and Castruccio's brave.
It is a desperate game that I must try,
And yet our only chance. There's little time,
But haste is the friend of enterprise:
I will but snatch a moment with Bianca,
Then to my task.

[Exit.

SCENE II

Interior of a Church.

CLARICHA enters, and makes an Offering of Flowers at the Shrine of the Madonna.

CLARICHA [Solus]
Lady divine, who yet art bound to earth
By the strong tie of sorrows shared, look down
And smile upon the offering which each day
I offer for his sake; if yet on earth,
Weary he wander, strengthen and support;
If thought of me add to his happiness
Keep it alive, and if it be regret,
Let me fade gently, like a pleasant dream—

Sweet, but too faint to rest on memory!
If—but, oh, no, not even in my prayers
Can I name death.—

[Sound of approaching steps.

Some one approaches, and I cannot bear
My quiet moment broken—

[She retires up the stage.

[Enter **CASTRUCCIO** muffled, and a Florentine **SPY**.

CASTRUCCIO
I understand their plan;
Florence will aid the strongest.

FLORENTINE
Such is her policy; her wishes take her
Upon the noble's side.

CASTRUCCIO
It matters not—
One victory more, and I can name my terms;
It is the secret stratagem I seek;
For that I look to thee—henceforth we meet
Within this church; few ever come this way.

FLORENTINE
To-morrow look for tidings from the camp.

CASTRUCCIO
I or Cesario will meet you here
At this same hour. Here is your promised gold.

FLORENTINE
Thanks; I will be secret as the grave.

Exit.

CASTRUCCIO
I loathe the tools that I perforce must use;
For sooner would I hang yon knave than pay him.
Crime takes no shape so base as treachery,
And yonder slave betrays his city's council
For a few ducats; but the time will come,
When, strong in Lucca's cause, I shall not need
Such an unworthy means; the slave and spy

Belong to tyranny, and freedom works
With nobler instruments.

[Going out, **CLARICHA** returns, they meet face to face, and recognize each other.

CASTRUCCIO
My loved, my lost, my beautiful Claricha!

CLARICHA
Oh! wake me not, Amino, if I dream.

CASTRUCCIO
Amino! how that name recalls my youth!
But whence art thou? when last I sought our home,
There was no vestige of the humble roof
That was the shelter of our early years.
I only found a heap of blacken'd ashes
O'er which the green weeds had begun to trail.

CLARICHA
You had not left us but a few sad months,
When, burnt and plunder'd by the Florentines,
Our village 'mid its vineyards lay in ruins;
The aid from Lucca sent, arrived too late
To save our homes; but to the chief Arrezi
I owe my life, and, placed by him, I dwelt
Long with a noble lady of his house,
Who loved me like the children she had lost.

CASTRUCCIO
The Count Arrezi! strange we never met.

CLARICHA
I have not been three days in Lucca—death
Left me once more alone in this cold world.
Again the Count Arrezi was my friend,
And placed me with his daughter, who is soon
To wed the Count Castruccio.

CASTRUCCIO
I am he.

CLARICHA
Amino!

CASTRUCCIO
Oh, breathe that name again—let it recall
All that my youth once dream'd of hope and love!

Or rather let me hear that name no more,
It is the death-knell of all happiness.

CLARICHA
Alas, I dare not question; yet, one word—
Have you forgotten me?

CASTRUCCIO
Forgotten what was dearest to my soul!

CLARICHA
Alas, how may that be, if Count Castruccio
And my Amino be the same?

CASTRUCCIO
Evil and bitter were my early years:
Exiled in childhood, sought for but to slay,
I only re-assumed our ancient name,
When, gathering all the remnants of our cause,
I raised the banner of our line, and came
A conqueror—who but only came to spare.

CLARICHA
I would that I had earlier known your name.

CASTRUCCIO
How bitterly I mock the pride that kept
My birth a secret; yet 'twas not all pride,
I plann'd a glad surprise for her I loved;
In the first dawn of my success, I sought
The well-remember'd vineyards.

CLARICHA
Farewell, Count Castruccio! had I known
The name whose triumphs fill our Italy,
I had not hoped as I have done for years;
But I should still have loved: it does not need
That words should say, the nameless, friendless girl
Is nothing to the Lord of Lucca.

CASTRUCCIO
Weary and hard has been my path through life;
Its brief success by danger has been bought,
Yet knew I not its bitterness till now.

CLARICHA
Farewell, my lord.

CASTRUCCIO

Hear me, Claricha—be yourself my judge—
What Lucca was, let our first years recall:
Years past in war and exile—when the land
Had not one vineyard safe—one hearth secure—
How stands my country now?—at peace within,
The peasant, undisturb'd beneath his vine,
The citizen in safety, high or low,
While our fair banners flout the gates of Florence.
Not for the palace only have I ruled,
But for the green fields and the market place;
Peace dwells beneath the shadow of my power.

CLARICHA

Ah, me! I know too well how much Castruccio
Has done for Lucca.

CASTRUCCIO

I have given youth,
And love, and hope, to be her sacrifice.
From the first hour that Lucca own'd my sway,
I only look'd to her prosperity:
The heart went with her that now turns aside;
On one side dost thou stand and happiness,
But on the other, danger, toil, and care.

CLARICHA

And duty!

CASTRUCCIO

A heavy duty girdles me around;
Arrezi's daughter has my plighted honour:
For Lucca's sake was the alliance sought,
To bind her father's party to my side.
A darker power than mine impels me on—
For the first time I hesitate, and fain
I would recall my purpose.

CLARICHA

Not for me;
Look on yon heaven, Castruccio, and think
Of thine own glorious future.

CASTRUCCIO

Has life no service I could render thee?

CLARICHA

What is there I could ask of thee but love?

CASTRUCCIO

I cannot part with thee: I had forgotten
That there were sweet and gentle thoughts in life;
Let me do something for thy sake, my loved one.

CLARICHA

Oh, death, this is thy agony!

CASTRUCCIO

The council will have met—I must away;
Who could restrain my followers in their fear
If I were missing? but not yet farewell,
I have so much to say, so much to ask.
We meet again, Claricha; I must seek
At least to be thy friend; we meet again.

CLARICHA

Alas! why should we meet? it is in vain.

CASTRUCCIO

I cannot choose, my heart beats quick with joy:
Youth, hope, and tenderness return with thee.

CLARICHA

For thine own sake, Castruccio, fare-thee-well.

CASTRUCCIO

Stay yet one moment; if thou didst but know
How faithfully this heart has kept thy name,
Its sad and secret music; years have past
Since the green vineyards heard our youthful vow;
Hurried our parting word, and parting kiss,
But not less sacred. In my first career
Thou wert my hope, my star of enterprise—
When I look'd forward, 'twas to look to thee.

CLARICHA

And now we meet, and know that we must part,
Unpitying fate! why met we not before?

CASTRUCCIO

My exile was repeal'd, but ere I sought
My native city, I did seek for thee;
Instead of sunny welcome in thine eyes,
I found but desolation and despair:
Dark night, and its eternal echoes, gave
The only answer when I call'd thy name.

CLARICHA

Oh! if we had but met.

CASTRUCCIO

Fate mocks at us; a few brief hours suffice
To stand between us and our happiness,
Thenceforth I had those gentle hopes no more,
That make the spirit gentle where they dwell.
Lucca was then my all—I had no hopes
But for the glory of my native city;
To see her free and prosperous, became
Life's sole great object.

CLARICHA

Not for my sake shall Lucca's hero pause
Upon his glorious path; not for my sake
Forget life's noblest duties.

CASTRUCCIO

Thou art more strong than I am—yet not so,
I see thy cheek is pale, thine eye is wet,
I cannot leave thee.

[Enter **CESARIO** hastily.

CESARIO

I pray your pardon, but the need is great;
The late attempt fills all your friends with fear,
Not mine to check their angry eagerness,
Which now is fain to seek thee, sword in hand.

CASTRUCCIO

To stay is madness now; my brief delay
May be atoned in blood. Love, now farewell.

CESARIO

I pray you, lady, urge his speed.

CLARICHA

Farewell! farewell!

CASTRUCCIO

Meet me again, Claricha, meet me here;
Here, with high Heaven, and the dead around,
Fit for farewell like ours. Sternly I feel
The pressure of my duty to the land,
Whose people are entrusted to my keeping;

But I cannot part with thee, and know so little
Of thy uncall'd-for future.

CESARIO
Good, my lord.

CASTRUCCIO
Claricha, most beloved, I dare not stay,
With life on every moment, bid me go.

CLARICHA
Farewell.

CASTRUCCIO
We meet to-morrow; every gentle saint
Watch over thee. Farewell.—

[Exeunt.

CLARICHA [Stands looking after him, and then turns suddenly and kneels before the Madonna]
At least I still may pray for him.—

ACT III

SCENE I —A Banqueting Hall opening into a garden, and hung with pictures.—

SERVANTS, COUNT AREZZI.

ARREZI [Solus]
I have but little heart for this gay banquet:
Dangers and fears encompass me around;
I know the Castrucani doubts my faith,
I know Leoni loathes the coming marriage.
Which never will his fiery spirit see
Without a struggle; and with that must come
All that I thought to shun of strife and blood.
Ah! there are moments, when my thoughts have ask'd
The heart that beats with them—can this be life?
This gulf of troubled waters, where the soul,
Like a vex'd bark, is toss'd upon the waves
Of pain and pleasure, by the warring breath
Of passions, like the winds that drive it on,
And only to distraction.—

[Sees **CLARICHA** coming from the garden.

Ah! she comes;
The gentle orphan, whose sweet sight more soothes
My troubled soul, than aught in this wide world.
I love her, for I know she needs my love,
And something in her sadness suits with mine.

[Enter **CLARICHA**

Welcome, my child! but how is this—the tears
Are in thine eyes Sweet one, why hast thou wept?

CLARICHA
My spirits are not good, my lord.

ARREZI
Thou art full young for sadness.

CLARICHA
Ah, my lord,
'Tis not the old alone who know that life
Has but a weary way.

ARREZI
My gentle child—
For ev'n as a child art thou to me—
Our life has many sorrows: and I think
Most bitterly is sorrow felt in youth.
Age comes and brings indifference: I grieve
Not as I used to grieve—I know the worst
Is but a painful dream that soon must pass.

CLARICHA
Would I could think so!

ARREZI
Believe me, maiden, could we read the past
In every heart, we should recoil to find
What weight of misery has been endured.

CLARICHA
Ah me! unequal are the lots in life.

ARREZI
More nearly are they balanced than we deem;
The outward life shows not the life within.
I am about to welcome in these walls
The Count Castruccio, and he is received
As the affianced lover of my daughter;

The crowd will only see the pomp and power,
And know not how the irrevocable past
Rises in all its darkness on my soul.
I hate the Castrucani's iron house.

CLARICHA
Hate them, my lord?

ARREZI
Is it the sadness in those gentle eyes
That suits my mood? but in thee, my fair child,
Is that which, winning on my confidence,
Soothes the old sorrow which it seems to share.
Since that first hour, when but a trembling girl
I met thee flying from the Florentines,
My heart warm'd to thee as thou wert my own.
Perhaps it is that in thy face and voice
There is a touch that brings again the face,
The voice, that once made heaven on earth to me.
'Twas but a dream of youth!

CLARICHA
Can such dreams pass?

ARREZI
Oh, never wholly can they be forgotten:
Good cause have I to hate the Castrucani!
I loved the loveliest lady of their line,
And wedded her in secret. Brief the space
That fate allow'd our moonlit happiness—
We were surprised together. From that hour
A settled darkness hangs upon her fate.
The drug or dagger did their fatal work
So secretly, that not a trace was left.
A dungeon was my share—for three long years
They held me captive, I escaped the third,
But never could I learn my lady's doom!

CLARICHA
Ah! such a parting well might break the heart.

ARREZI
Time brings strange chances, when a child of mine
Weds with the Castrucani—but in vain
Age seeks to struggle with its destiny;
I'm worn and weary—all I seem to wish
Is but a little rest before I die.

CLARICHA
Speak not so mournfully, my own kind friend,
Think how affection girdles you around,
How gratitude puts up its prayer to heaven,
Whene'er the orphan names Arrezi's name.

ARREZI
My own sweet child, would thou wert truly mine!
I've sadden'd where at first we meant to cheer.
We'll talk of grief no more; I pray you cast
Your eye around, and see that all be set
In fair array. I must now seek Leoni—

[Going.

I had forgotten what I meant to say—
You and Bianca must be brave to-night.
I bade my pages carry to your chamber
Some toys and gauds I trust will please your fancy.

CLARICHA
You are too kind.

ARREZI
Nay, I am only glad
To give so slight a pleasure.

[Exit.

CLARICHA
It is in vain—I cannot fix my thoughts
On aught but him. Amino, no, Castruccio!
How have I pray'd for years that we might meet—
We meet, and only meet to part for ever.
I know not what I look upon—all things
Repeat his likeness—I can hear his voice,
Or is it but the beating of my heart?
The Count Leoni here? Let me escape,
I could not bear his idle gallantry.—

[Looks round.

This column will conceal me.

[Enter the **COUNT LEONI**, followed by **ARREZI**.

ARREZI
It is too desperate!

LEONI
So are our fortunes!
We are the ladders of Castruccio's greatness,
Used, then flung down.

ARREZI
Nay, we must rise with him.

LEONI
One of our noble house should scorn such rise;
Ancestral is our hatred, dark with time!
And seal'd on either side with blood. To-day
Cannot undo the work of many years.

ARREZI
Where are the well-laid schemes of yesterday?

LEONI
Lost by your own weak fears: he should have died.
Castruccio's only prison is the grave!

ARREZI
But still to slay him—coming as my guest
In my own halls—

LEONI
The strong may choose their time,
The weak take opportunity to strike.

ARREZI
I cannot—dare not.

LEONI
Dare not, is the word;
I'll dare for both. Now listen, uncle mine;
Bianca is my own betrothed bride!
Castruccio shall not wed her; that alone
Were cause enough to float these halls with blood:
He is our house's ancient enemy,
And, but for him, no citizen would dare
Raise hand against the nobles; he must die!

ARREZI
But yet some fitter time.

LEONI
The hour for action is the present hour!

Defeat and danger wait upon delay.
Castruccio will be here to-night, unarm'd,
His surest friends beside him; they will fall,
None to avenge. Our friends are all prepared;
A secret band of Florentines now lie
In ambush by the city's western gate,
Whose keeper I have gain'd. I haste to seek them
Bearing the orders of the Count Gonsalvi,
Who'll meet them at the gate and lead them on.
Castruccio slain—the people overawed,
Henceforth our triumph is secure.

ARREZI
It will be bought too dearly.

LEONI
Danger will only heighten our success.

ARREZI
'Tis not the danger, 'tis the treachery.

LEONI
I've heard the treachery of the Castrucani
Gave you three years of prison in your youth.

ARREZI
Do not recall that bitter time again.

LEONI
I must recall its memory—let it cry
For vengeance at our hands. I will away;
Short time is mine to reach the Florentines,
And yet return to grace the festival:
My entrance at the banquet is the signal!

ARREZI
Castruccio may miss you from the halls
Whose heir should be the first to bid him welcome!

LEONI
A little colouring gives truth to falsehood,
Tell him I'm jealous of Bianca's smile.

ARREZI
But—

LEONI
Buts are the stumbling-blocks of enterprise,

We will not have them.

ARREZI
The risk is fearful—do not think Castruccio
Will yield without a struggle. How can I
Stand by and see him murder'd?

LEONI
Out on such scruples! Hear me, Count Arrezi!
Go to Castruccio's feet, and tell him all;
Give up your kinsmen and your ancient friends,
And henceforth be his vassal. For ourselves,
We are prepared to die, though not prepared
To perish by your act.

ARREZI
You know no death could tempt me to betray you.

LEONI
You have your choice—his life or ours!

ARREZI
Leoni, I am now a man in years,
Broken and wayworn, and I lack the force
To lead or stem the tide of your fierce spirits;
On either hand is death!

LEONI
That of your friends and foes is at your choice.

ARREZI
I have no choice.

LEONI
Then, neither can you be responsible.
But now I must away—time hurries on,
One parting word—be calm and resolute.

[Exit.

ARREZI
Hear me one moment more!

[Follows him.

CLARICHA [Coming forward]
Thank God, I have heard all! oh, give me strength
To fly and save him!

[Exit.

SCENE II

A small Chamber looking to the Street.

Enter **CLARICHA**, hastily.

CLARICHA
All egress is forbidden from the palace,
They will not let me forth, and he must die!
I must behold him murder'd in my sight!
Can I not watch, when first he comes, and speak
At once my words of warning in his ear?
Too late, the armed traitors will be nigh:
Can I not save him? I, who would lay down
My life to save him? Pitying heaven, look down
And aid me in this hopeless misery.
[After a pause]
These windows look upon the street—a scroll
Might save him yet—it is a desperate chance!
Still, if it reach his hand, he were in safety.

[She approaches the table, and writes.

Be still, thou coward hand! thou shalt not tremble.

[She writes.

'Tis done—these few brief words suffice
To warn Castruccio of the coming danger.

[She folds the letter.

Holy Madonna, have it in thy care!

[She attempts to throw it out, the wind blows it back again.

'Tis too light—'twill never reach the street;

[She looks anxiously round.

It should be heavy—heavy as my heart!
Oh, nothing!—nothing, if I had but here

One of those daggers soon to drink his blood!

[Suddenly recollecting, she puts her hand to her throat.

'Tis here, the chain I have from childhood worn!
My only relic of the unknown past.
But let it go—it will weigh down the scroll—

[She makes up the packet.
Now heav'n speed it that it reach Castruccio!

[She flings it from the window.

It falls—I see it lying in the street.
Now all depends on who may find it first.
Star of his glorious hour, send thou some friend!
Let but a noble pass, and he is lost!
A common citizen draws near the spot;
He sees the packet—takes it—reads the name,
And hurries to the Castrucani palace.
I know yon street leads straight unto its gates;
Oh God, I thank thee!

[Sinks exhausted by the window.

SCENE III

A Hall in one of the Palaces.

LEONI, and SEVERAL NOBLES

1st NOBLE
I would you had been with us yesterday.

LEONI
To-day will serve us better; for to-day
Has yesterday's experience.

1st NOBLE
We were wrong
To trust the people and the light of day;
Now secret night is round our enterprise,
And we will be as secret.

LEONI
All now rests

Upon your own good swords and with yourselves.

2nd NOBLE
If that the matter rested with my sword
I were content—that were a soldier's part.
Midnight assassins are we now!

LEONI
Actions are ever judged by their success;
To-morrow sees us paramount in Lucca;
The doom to-night dealt on the Castrucani
Will then be rightful justice

1st NOBLE
We have no choice: it is his fall or ours,
And I, for one, care little if my sword
Or if my dagger end an enemy.

LEONI
We are degraded by the Castrucani;
Our order has not left one privilege
Beyond the meanest citizen.

2nd NOBLE
He talks, too, of dismissing our retainers.

LEONI
'Tis the old fable of the lion's claws,
But we must re-assert our ancient rule;
Assert it now or never, for I know
The emperor's envoys are upon their way
To own the Castrucani Lord of Lucca,
But they must find us masters!

1st NOBLE
Your entrance at the banquet is our signal?

LEONI
Yes, and I ask one favour; let my dagger
Be that which strikes Castruccio!

ALL
Agreed!

LEONI
Our time is precious; to your care, Count Ludolph,
I will commend my uncle: he is old,
And weak, and fearful—see he falter not.

You, Count Rinaldo, have our followers arm'd,
And meet me secret in the cypress-grove;
I'll wait there, coming from the Florentines.
Our forces and their band must join at once;
This fix'd, we'll seek the banquet-room together.
My welcome to Castruccio is my dagger!

1st NOBLE
One cup of wine, Leoni, ere you go.

LEONI
I have not time—yet stay—we'll drink one pledge.

[They pour out wine; each takes a goblet.

Death to the Castrucani!

ALL
Death to the Castrucani!

LEONI
And now away—away—for life and death
Is on the hour!

[Exeunt.

ACT IV

SCENE I —The same Hall as before, but now illuminated, hung with Pictures, &c.

COUNT ARREZI, BIANCA, CLARICHA, GUESTS, &c.

CLARICHA anxiously watching the groups as they enter.

ARREZI
Welcome, my friends!

[After two or three greetings.

[Aside]
We cannot now recede, they come prepared.

CLARICHA [Aside]
He comes not!

1st NOBLE

You've spared, good count, no cost upon your banquet.
[Aside]
Wear not that moody brow, to-night is ours.

ARREZI [Aside]
Alas! that this must be.—
[Aloud]
—The count is late.

1st NOBLE
We're used to wait the Count Castruccio's pleasure.

CLARICHA [Aside]
Perhaps he may not come!

ARREZI
Fair ladies, will you dance?

[A dance.

CLARICHA [Aside]
Each moment gives me hope he may not come.

ARREZI
You stand apart; will you not dance my child?

CLARICHA
I am not well.
[Aside]
—Oh, Heaven, he comes!

[Enter **CASTRUCCIO, CESARIO,** and **ATTENDANTS.**

ARREZI
Welcome, my noble guest!

CLARICHA [Aside]
The chain is round his neck.

CASTRUCCIO
Thanks for your courtesy. The fair Bianca!

BIANCA
You're welcome, signor.

1st NOBLE [Aside]
The victim, now, is safe within our toils!

ARREZI
You're late, my lord.

CASTRUCCIO
I pray your pardon, 'twas no fault of mine!

1st NOBLE
It was our pride and pleasure to expect.

CLARICHA [Aside]
I see he is prepared; his eagle eye
Flashes, as, when a boy, he spoke of danger.

[Enter **SERVANT**.

The banquet waits, my lord.

ARREZI [Aside]
There can be no delay,

1st NOBLE [Aside]
And no misgiving!

ARREZI
Our banquet's ready. Please you, Count Castruccio,
To lead Bianca?

CASTRUCCIO
Your pardon, lady, for a brief delay;
Let me look round this hall, I knew it not.

ARREZI
'Tis never open'd but when some high guest
Honours us with his presence; and we ask
Our ancestors to aid us in his greeting.

CASTRUCCIO
I like the custom. It is from the dead
The living must their noblest lessons learn;
The dead are as the stars that light the past:
We see how time has honoured them, and hope
Ourselves for equal honour.

1st NOBLE
True my good lord.
[Aside to **ARREZI**]
Why dost thou look so scared?

CASTRUCCIO
The name of every noble ancestor's
A bond upon the soul against disgrace!
'Tis no vain pride that looketh to their honours,
And taketh thence a high security
That we prove not unworthy of such names.

ARREZI [Aside]
I cannot bear this.
[Aloud]
The banquet waits!

CASTRUCCIO
A little while, I pray you, let it wait.
I like this gallery much—our history,
Our Lucca's history, is on its walls;
Her noblest, and her bravest, and her best,
Keep the time-honour'd life of memory.
Now, if a man had plann'd some low vile deed,
He dared not act it here.

1st NOBLE [Aside]
Can he suspect?
[Aloud]
Some men are resolute.

CASTRUCCIO
Yonder is one who reign'd our doge in Lucca;
'Tis now some fifty years—I know the face.
The public monument the public raised
In gratitude for a long life of service.
His statue looks upon the town he ruled,
An honour unto both. It is the past
Redeems the present, and that bids us look
To the dim future with a lofty hope.
Cold and unworthy were the actual hours,
If they look'd only to themselves; but life
Is conscious of its immortality,
Urged by high duty—animate by power;
The present, in the shadow of the past,
Learns what it owes the future.
The sage, the hero, leave their great example
Heroic guides upon a glorious path;
They are the lights by which we shape our course,
Only by looking up can we see Heav'n.

1st NOBLE
You're eloquent, my lord!

ARREZI [Aside]

I'll try to save him, and must see Leoni
[Aloud]
Our guests await your pleasure.

CASTRUCCIO
I pray their pardon: but who is yon knight
Clad in white armour?

ARREZI
Our house's chiefest honour; when the Moors
Made him a prisoner, on his plighted word,
So high they held the Count Vitelli's name,
They let him seek his native land to raise
The ransom which they set. He found his lands
Impoverish'd like the state, and could not raise
The heavy sum required. In vain 'twas urged
Small faith was needed with the Infidel;
But he return'd, taking his chains again,
And died a captive.

CASTRUCCIO
And, in the presence of this noble knight,
Who looks in visible scorn upon ye now,
Your ancestor, Arrezi, have you plann'd
To violate all hospitable rites!

ARREZI
Count Castruccio!

CASTRUCCIO
A cowardly assassin; but in vain.

[He stamps; his **GUARD** comes in.

1st NOBLE
We sell our lives full dearly!

[Springs at **CASTRUCCIO**, who strikes his sword from his hand.

CASTRUCCIO
Take them to prison; ladies, by your leave,
This is no place for you.

[Addressing one of them.

Madam, I give the Count Arrezi's daughter
To your kind charge and honourable keeping;
We never meet again!

[Exeunt.

[**CLARICHA** comes forward.

CASTRUCCIO [Not knowing her]
Lady, I crave your absence.

CLARICHA
I only stay to ask my chain again.

CASTRUCCIO [Recognising her]
Your chain! My own Claricha, have you been
Lucca's good angel—sweet preserver, mine!
Take back your chain, and, with it, take my heart
And its entire allegiance. Oh! sweet love,
This is no time to pour my heart in words,
Yet happiness must ask a moment's space.
Saved, and by thee!

CLARICHA
Ah! would I not lay down my life for thine

CASTRUCCIO
Like a good angel's gift I hold the life
Which thou hast rescued; it must be for good:
Life's sweetest hopes return again with thee.
Mine once again—my own, long lost Claricha!
This very evening I reproach'd my fate;
To meet thee still the beautiful, the true,
And yet resign thee, was too hard a task!
I question'd with my honour, and I falter'd
In the stern path of right: but I am now
So happy, my Claricha!

CLARICHA
Would I might ever make thy happiness!

CASTRUCCIO
One word—where does my sweet one make her home?

CLARICHA
With Count Arrezi.

CASTRUCCIO

With mine enemy!

CLARICHA
No longer such; henceforward bound to thee
By a free pardon.

CASTRUCCIO
I cannot pardon him.

CLARICHA
Not pardon him, Castruccio, for my sake?

CASTRUCCIO
I cannot pardon him for Lucca's sake!

CLARICHA
One moment hear me: oh! Castruccio, think
How kind the count has been; my one true friend!
An orphan—pity was my only claim;
It was enough with him—I owe him all
Of fond affection's care; but for that care
I were not here to kneel and ask for mercy.

CASTRUCCIO
Kneel not to me; ah! listen, dearest mine!

CLARICHA
Will you not pay my debt of gratitude?

CASTRUCCIO
Ask for my life, Claricha, it is thine!
But ask not for the lives which others trust
Safe to my charge; think not that I refuse
Arrezi's life because he sought for mine;
I have no anger for my private wrong:
But there are those in Lucca who need warning,
And they shall have it. With the traitor's head
A thousand plots fall harmless from the scaffold.

CLARICHA
Nothing disarms an enemy like pardon.

CASTRUCCIO
Not when they think the pardon wrung from fear.
Ancient oppression—present treachery—
Alike demand example. At our gates
Gather the foreign foe; they must not hope
For aid within our walls: I have long tried

A gentle rule of patience—'tis no more.
Plead not with those sad eyes, the count must die!

CLARICHA
I do implore you by our ancient love!

CASTRUCCIO
Oh! do not think that when I take this hand
I link it to a calm and happy lot;

You will share with me sacrifice and pain.
For power, it is an awful thing, and stands
Girt by stern duties. Not to thy sweet tears
May I yield up one staid and solemn purpose;
Once have I pardon'd: but, to pardon twice,
Were weakness, and not mercy. He must die!

CLARICHA
Castruccio!

CASTRUCCIO
Not where my heart has chosen must it find
Unrest and womanish complaint; weep, love,
Kindly and natural tears; but still remember
Lucca has my first duty. Cesario, wait.
Farewell, love! within a few short hours
We'll meet again; when I shall ask from thee
More justice to mine act.

[Exit.

CLARICHA
It is my hand has slain him; he, my friend,
My kind—my only friend. Is there no hope?
I did not urge him earnestly enough—
I did not tell him he would lose my love
Unless he heard my desperate pray'rs for mercy.
Oh! never shall I know a quiet hour
Again in life, unless Arrezi live;
His memory will haunt me like a ghost,
Pale and perpetual at my side, with eyes
That never turn aside their sad reproach.
I'll after him, and wring a slow consent.

CESARIO
Your pardon, lady; do not seek the count,
Let his just anger cool; think you how false,
How vile has been Arrezi's part to-night!

With flattering words he pray'd Castruccio's presence,
Made his own child the lure, yet, in his heart,
Lurk'd the assassin, and he plann'd to make
His home—his sacred home—the place for murder!

CLARICHA
It is too true—but he was urged by others.

CESARIO
Lady, it does not justify our crime,
Saying that others prompted us to sin.

CLARICHA
Alas! alas! I cannot think of him
But as he was to me—a kind old man,
The only friend my orphan girlhood knew.
Oh! I must see him; I must kneel and weep
Before his feet—he cannot pardon me—
Yet let me ask forgiveness. Gentle youth,
Conduct me to the prison.

CESARIO
'Twill need an order to allow your entrance.

CLARICHA
Seek ye Castruccio; he will not refuse,
And I, meanwhile, must weep and pray. Oh! Fate,
How thou dost mock us! I have met Castruccio,
The prayer of many years has been fulfill'd;
We love with that true love we vow'd at parting,
Yet my full heart sinks down with misery.
My kind—my only friend—oh! gentle youth,
Haste, for sweet pity's sake.

[Exeunt.

SCENE II

Part of a Garden.

LEONI pacing backwards and forwards.

LEONI
There is no cloud upon the placid sky,
There is no motion in the drooping leaves;
I neither like this waiting nor this stillness.

Too much the rest of this still night contrasts
The unrest that is feverish in my soul!
The midnight, with its pale and mournful moon,
That wanders, like an orphan, through the heavens,
Companionless, with its dark boughs, that seem
Still as the heavy shadows which they fling,
This hour is not for enterprise. The heart
Mocks its own projects and its own designs,
So little, with eternal night around,
So worthless, gazing on those distant worlds.
Why, what vain fantasies are these to cross
My mind at such a time! but we are toys
E'en to ourselves. Where can Rinaldo stay?
The banquet hour is past—Ah! here he comes.

[Enter **2nd NOBLE** hastily.

You come full late, my lord

2nd NOBLE
I come too soon;
Despair and danger are my comrades here!

LEONI
What can you mean?

2nd NOBLE
Mean? that Castruccio's friend
Has stood him in good stead; he came prepared,
Knowing the welcome that he was to meet.
Your uncle and his friends are now in prison,
Condemn'd to death.

LEONI
The Count Arrezi prisoner!

2nd NOBLE
Aye—and his shadow falls upon his grave,
He stands so near to it. Just now I pass'd
Beside the market-place; the midnight rang
With the loud hammer's blow, and with the saw
Grating its sullen pathway through the wood
Which is to raise the scaffold for to-morrow.
Arrezi there will be the first to die.

LEONI
Not if my life can ransom his. 'Twas I
Who urged the old man on—with sneer and threat

I silenced his misgivings.

2nd NOBLE
What can we do?

LEONI
Rather than let that old man die, I'd kneel
Before the Castrucani, and give up
My head as fitting ransom.

2nd NOBLE
You would but only add another victim.
We have no choice but flight.

LEONI
I will not fly,
Though I but stay'd to share Arrezi's scaffold.

2nd NOBLE
Live for revenge—a better hour may come.

LEONI
Revenge is all too distant; I will save
Or perish!

2nd NOBLE
I tell you all is known; what can avail
A single arm?

LEONI
Tis to that single arm that I must trust.
There yet remains one sole—one desperate chance—
The risk is mine.
[Drawing his dagger]
This blade has stood, ere now,
My certain friend.
[Sheathing it]
—I'll trust to it again.

2nd NOBLE
Castruccio's guards are gather'd round his palace;
And, if some cunning tale could win your entrance,
You'd perish, ev'n as you struck the blow.
A hundred swords would straight avenge his death.

LEONI
I'd brave them all, Rinaldo, in such cause;
But mine's a far more subtle stratagem.

2nd NOBLE

Your stratagems have not avail'd us much.

LEONI

The chances of the game have turn'd against us,
And I will pay the forfeit with my head,
Unless I turn them yet again.

2nd NOBLE

There's something in your courage raises mine;
I'll follow you.

LEONI

That suits not with my scheme: take you this ring,
And hurry with it to the Florentines,
Who lay in ambush near the ruin'd tower;
Hasten their march; I did not wish their aid
Until our party muster'd in its strength:
But now, our life and death hangs on their speed.
Hence, good Rinaldo.

2nd NOBLE

Not till I know your purpose for yourself.
Half of the danger is my proper share.

LEONI

On my right hand alone I must rely.
You may remember, in our boyish days
My father held the Castrucani palace—
The Castrucani were themselves in exile;
I know each turn and winding—there was one,
A secret passage leading to the city,
And from the very room which now Castruccio
Makes his own private chamber—leave that way,
And, Fortune, I will worship thee again.

2nd NOBLE

Methinks that Fortune owes us some amends
For past ill-favour.

LEONI

We must away; each moment that we lose
Brings my old kinsman nearer to the scaffold.
Off to the Florentines! Now life and death
Hang on an hour's chance.

[Exeunt different ways.

ACT V

SCENE I—A Prison

ARREZI and the **CONFESSOR**.

ARREZI
Thou bring'st my youth again; thou who didst link
Her faith to mine—the lost and the beloved.
Fateful to me has been thy ministering;
It has been thine, oh! ancient priest, to bless
My marriage and my scaffold!

CONFESSOR
Not on the past, my son, fix thou thy thoughts,
But on the solemn future!

ARREZI
I cannot choose: I sought thee out for years.
Give me to know her fate—my secret bride—
Soon lost, but long beloved—and I will turn
From thee to thy companion—death!

CONFESSOR
When the proud Castrucani forced thy bride
To secret banishment, and made thee prisoner,
Chance brought me to the village, and I watch'd
Above her and her child—

ARREZI
Her child!

CONFESSOR
It was two years before the mother died;
With her last breath she gave her to my charge.

ARREZI
What of the orphan?

CONFESSOR
For years I saw her grow in loveliness,
And deem'd her happy in her lowly state;
For Lucca was distracted with the wars
Her nobles kept among themselves.

ARREZI

I dread—yet still must ask—does my child live?

CONFESSOR

But that it breaks a link with this sad world,
My heart would fail me—no, the girl is dead!
She had just sprung to blooming womanhood,
When Heaven claim'd its own. The Florentines
Burnt Arola, the village where she dwelt;
Not one escaped to tell the tale of death!

ARREZI

Oh, subtle force of nature's secret love!
That child, although I knew her not for mine,
Has been my care; I have reproach'd myself
That more my heart drew to her than Bianca:
Our house almost enforced my second marriage.
I wedded with a lady cold and proud,
Who left her likeness to her child—Bianca
Ne'er sought, ne'er won affection like Claricha;
Would I might bless her ere I die.

CONFESSOR

Alas! my son, think not on human ties.

[Enter **CLARICHA**

ARREZI

And hast thou sought me out, my own sweet child?
Come to your father's heart! 'twas Heaven and nature
That made me love thee, ere I knew thy right
To claim a parent's love. How hard it is
To only know thee in this last sad hour!
Shrink not away, my child—I am thy father!

CLARICHA

My father!

CONFESSOR

She wears the very chain around her neck
Placed by her dying mother. Start not thus,
But kneel and ask a father's latest blessing.

CLARICHA

Mercy—mercy.

ARREZI

In evil times we meet; but still, my child,
Come to my heart—Claricha, let me bless thee!

CLARICHA
Curse me—your blessing sinks me to the earth:
Curse me—and in me curse your murderer!

ARREZI
Cease these wild words, you know not what you say.

CLARICHA
I know too well: I gave the Count Castruccio
The tidings of his danger.

ARREZI
You told Castruccio!

CONFESSOR
Unhappy girl!

CLARICHA
I told Castruccio—in our early youth
We met and loved; the burning of our village
Lost us each other's trace; again we met—
That very day I overheard your scheme,
And gave him warning.

ARREZI
I cannot blame thee.

CLARICHA
He loves me—oh! he cannot let me die—
Die with a parent's blood upon my soul!
He did not know of this—yes, there is hope.

ARREZI
Hope!

CLARICHA
My father—let me call thee by that name—
My father, bless me—bless thy wretched child!
Oh, try to say one word of comfort to me!
I come to seek thy pardon.

[Kneels.

ARREZI
I blame our evil destiny, and feel

'Tis my own crime has brought down Heaven's vengeance;
I dare not say I pardon thee, Claricha,
But take thy father's blessing; my last prayer
Shall be for thee!

CLARICHA
Either I bring thy pardon, or I die;
I seek Castruccio: never will I rise
From kneeling at his feet, until I win
Forgiveness for my father. Once, again,
I pray thee bless me.

ARREZI
Come to my heart?

[They embrace.

CLARICHA
Now, pitying Heaven assist me.—

[Exit.

CONFESSOR
Let us now seek the inner cell, and pray.

ARREZI
She must succeed; I feel
My heart beat quick with hope.—I follow thee.

[Exeunt.

SCENE II

CASTRUCCIO alone in his Chamber, writing.

CASTRUCCIO
There is a heavy weight upon my heart
That I would fling aside, yet cannot fling;
But that I hold all such presentments vain,
I should think there was evil on this hour.
Yet where should be the evil? yonder star
That brings the golden promise of the day,
Is, as my fortunes, rising to their noon.
Victory bears my crimson banner onwards;
Love nestles in its shadow; and, subdued,
Mine enemies are prostrate at my feet.

Bear witness, Lucca! in this silent hour,
That my first thought is thine; I have not ask'd
A transitory name for thee or me;
My conquests have but sought to keep our gates
Steadfast against a foreign foe; within
Have I kept order and security.
The iron power, made selfish by the few,
Have I subdued, and temper'd in its use.
The citizens have learnt to know their strength,
And in that strength lies freedom.

[The panel at the back begins to open, and **LEONI** appears. He advances towards **CASTRUCCIO**, who starts, but instantly composes himself, and appears occupied by the papers on the table.

CASTRUCCIO [Aside]
I hear the secret lock I thought none knew
Turn in the panel, and I hear a step;
It is too stealthy for a friendly one—
Let me be on my guard—it comes more near.
I see a shadow darken on the ground:
There is a dagger in the hand. I'll seem
Busy among these letters while I watch.

[**LEONI** attempts to stab him, but **CASTRUCCIO** springs up, and snatches the dagger.

CASTRUCCIO
The Count Leoni turn'd assassin?

[Throws down the dagger.

LEONI
Now curses on the worthless hand that fail'd
With life and honour trusted to its strength!

CASTRUCCIO
Honour! that is no word for lip of thine—
A coward murderer in the silent night.
Does not thy noble name cry shame upon thee?

LEONI
It cries for vengeance!

CASTRUCCIO
What cause hast thou to be my enemy?

LEONI
An hundred years our houses have been foes;
To that I add my individual hate.

There is no path of fortune where thy step
Has not cross'd mine; in war, ambition, love,
Still hast thou been my rival! call thy guards,
Tyrant! but, ere they come, I'll try my sword.

CASTRUCCIO
I'll call no other guard than my right hand.

[They fight.—As he disarms **LEONI**, **CESARIO** and the **ATTENDANTS** rush in.

CASTRUCCIO
Bear hence the traitor! you are just in time.

CESARIO
He bleeds to death.

LEONI
But yet with strength enough
For hatred and defiance; 'tis in vain—
Fate is against me—curse the hand and sword
That have betray'd me in my utmost need!
Yet hark, Castruccio! thou hast many foes—
Dagger and cup are armed against thy life!
And with my dying breath I bid them speed.
But I am dizzy—no—I dare not leave
Word for my kind old kinsman or Bianca:
Now can I neither save, nor yet revenge.

CESARIO
Die with more christian words upon your lips,
For the dear sake of thy immortal soul!

LEONI [Springing up for a moment]
I'll peril it on my last word—I hate him!

[Dies.

CASTRUCCIO
Bear him away, and instantly prepare
Arrezi's scaffold; I will make my power
Show itself fearful: they must learn my strength.

[Exeunt **ATTENDANTS** bearing the body.

CESARIO
Can you be hurt my lord? you look so pale.

CASTRUCCIO

I am more sad than is my wont, Cesario!
My hand has slain yon traitor, but he once
Was my familiar friend—yet scarce my friend,
For friendship asks as much as love—of faith—
Of mingling qualities and confidence;
Friends, then, we were not, but such gay companions
As are remember'd pleasant in our age;
They wear the freshness of our youth about them,
And bring back hours untramell'd by a care!
Many a midnight have we pass'd together
In glad carousal, when the purple cup
Gave its own gaiety; we've fought together,
'Neath the same banner was our earliest field!
We've sat beside the watch-fire half the night,
Talking of friends and of our native city,
Yet yonder doth he lie, slain by my hand!

CESARIO
Better ten thousand perish'd such as he,
Than peril life so dear as your's to Lucca.

CASTRUCCIO
Lucca—that is the watchword of my heart!
My native city! you are young, Cesario,
And do not know with how intense a love
The exile clingeth to his mother earth.
I was an exile once—and Lucca rose
Each night more beautiful among my dreams;
Each day a deeper longing seized my soul
To see her walls once more; at length I came,
And found disorder, tyranny and death!
It matters not to tell you of my youth;
Enough, it left me with no home-affection,
None of those gentler ties that fill the thoughts
Of other men—my country was my all!
My hopes, my fears, my future were for Lucca.

CESARIO
And you have made our Lucca what she is,
Peace in her streets, and victory at her gates.

CASTRUCCIO
I know my power—alas! I also know
Power is a sad and solitary thing;
It cuts you off from old companionship,
It needeth iron heart and iron eye,
For its resolves are terrible, when life
Waits on your word, and when you know one breath—

One little breath—takes what it cannot give!
I yield the Count Arrezi to the axe,
But have no word that could recall the blow!

CESARIO
His doom is just!

CASTRUCCIO
And needful; vain, indeed, my present mood—
Power must submit to its dark comrade—death!

[**ATTENDANT** enters.

A lady craves a moment's speech, my lord.

CASTRUCCIO
Let her approach: leave us awhile, Cesario.

[Exeunt.

I know the step:—

[Enter **CLARICHA**.

—my sweet lady here,
What would she ask?

CLARICHA
What thou hast once denied,
A pardon for Arrezi.

CASTRUCCIO
Let me entreat thy silence—grieve me not
With useless prayers I may not—dare not grant;
Thy hand is cold—your lip is white—sweet love,
For my sake, wear not such wild wretchedness.

CLARICHA
You cannot dream what misery brings me to you;
Hear me: it is my father's life I seek—
My father's!

CASTRUCCIO
What does this mean?

CLARICHA
You could not leave a crime upon my soul
So terrible! Arrezi is my parent!

CASTRUCCIO
Your parent! How is this?

CLARICHA
Secret he wedded one of your proud line
Who parted them, and never till this hour
Knew he his wife, nor yet his orphan's fate.
I am that wretched child!

CASTRUCCIO
Can this be true?

CLARICHA
Oh! do not cruelly waste time in doubt.
But let my agony attest the truth;
His life—my life—now hang upon a word.
Be merciful, Castruccio! speak that word,
Or see me die before you!

CASTRUCCIO
There is no doubt?

CLARICHA
None—none! Now, by our love, I do implore you!
He was my benefactor and my friend—
He is my father!

CASTRUCCIO
I cannot let her hand—her innocent hand—
Redden for ever with a parent's blood!
Nature, thy ties are sacred, and I yield.
Haste with my signet; love, your father lives,
And you shall be his hostage.

CLARICHA
Let my haste thank you. Oh! my noble lord,
Long years of happiness reward this pardon!

[Exit

[Tumult without. **CESARIO** and **OTHERS** rush in.

CESARIO
My lord, some treachery has been at work.
Through the west gate the Florentines have won
Their secret entrance, and the Count Gonsalvi
Raises his war-cry in our streets.

CASTRUCCIO
'Tis well;
Long have I sought to meet him face to face,
And now a single blow may end the war.

The Market-place.

CITIZENS, &c. Sound of tumult, and a bell tolling in the distance.

1st CITIZEN
They fly before Castruccio; but a band,
With Count Gonsalvi, keep the western gate.

2nd CITIZEN
They will not keep it long; the Florentines
Know our Castruccio.

1st CITIZEN
Did the prisoner pass
While I was gone?

2nd CITIZEN
The moment that you left;
I wait to see the body brought this way.

1st CITIZEN
Lo! where they come.

[The **CROWD** press together; and, as the body, covered on a bier, is brought in on one side, **CLARICHA** enters at the other. The bearers set down the body.

CLARICHA
I cannot urge my way—in Heaven's name,
I pray you, let me pass.

1st CITIZEN
Rest you a little while, poor child, beside me:
You cannot pierce the crowd.

CLARICHA
I must go on; oh, for your parents' sake
Make but a little way!

1st CITIZEN

The crowd will soon disperse—they pause to gaze
On Count Arrezi.

CLARICHA
Help me—I am his child—I bring his pardon.
Now, in your children's—in your fathers' name—
Let me pass on.

1st CITIZEN
It is too late.

[**CLARICHA** springs forward with a shriek, the **CROWD** give way, and she reaches the bier.

CLARICHA
Who lies beneath that mantle?

OFFICER
The traitor, Count Arrezi.

[**CLARICHA** drops by the bier. Flourish of trumpets, acclamations.

[Enter **CASTRUCCIO, GONSALVI**, Florentine **PRISONERS, SOLDIERS**, &c.

GONSALVI [Offering his sword to **CASTRUCCIO**]
Thus I yield up my sword as vanquish'd twice;
Once by your arm, more by your courtesy.

CASTRUCCIO
Keep it, my lord; and with it take your freedom:
We only ask of victory for peace.

[Enter **CESARIO**.

CESARIO
The envoys of the emperor await
Your leisure, to acknowledge you the lord
Of Lucca.

CASTRUCCIO
Then Lucca's freedom is assured. High Heaven
I thank thee!
[Addressing the **CROWD**]
My friends,
Not on a day of victory and peace,
Shall justice sternly ask its penalty
Freely ye will forgive your enemies.
Last night's conspirators I pardon here—
Be they set free.

OFFICER
That has been done by death!
There lies the Count Arrezi.

[The **CROWD** opens, and **CLARICHA** is seen lying by the bier.

CASTRUCCIO
Oh, miserable mockery of fate!
Look up, Claricha.

[She starts at his voice.

CLARICHA
His voice—ah! let it wake me from my dream.
I've had a fearful dream—Castruccio mine—
But I am safe, thus nestled in thine arms!

CASTRUCCIO [Attempting to bear her away]
Come with me, love—this is no place for thee.

CLARICHA [Springing from him]
Why am I here, and wherefore is this crowd?
There's fear in every face—they look on me
With pity or with horror, and your eyes
Are not familiar—ah! you turn aside—
Speak to me—smile as you once did, Castruccio—
Still do you turn away—what have I done?
There are too many here—I cannot ask you—
A strange confusion mixes up my thoughts,
And at my heart there is a faint sick pain.

CASTRUCCIO
Lean on me, love.

CLARICHA [Looking towards the bier]
Who are those men—those dark and fearful men?
What do the black folds of yon mantle hide?
I seem as I had look'd on them before;
There is a weight upon my struggling soul—
'Tis blood—my father's blood—
It is my father murder'd by his child!

[Sinks in **CASTRUCCIO'S** arms.

GONSALVI
Give way, the lady faints!

CASTRUCCIO

I tell you it is death—look up, my love!
Silence those trumpets; ah! she doth not hear.
Claricha—my Claricha—so long lost,
So lately found—youth—joy and hope are gone!
Gone, my pale beauty—we shall love no more!

CESARIO

Oh, come, my lord, all Lucca sees your tears!

CASTRUCCIO

Lucca should be their witness; for her sake—
For my fair country's sake—I have kept down
Natural emotions, young and cheerful thoughts,
Yet were they warm and eager at my heart.
With her they perish! Fate has claim'd the last,
Cruel and terrible the sacrifice!
All but my country shares Claricha's grave—

[Raising her in his arms.

This, Lucca, is my latest offering!

[The Curtain drops.